Gorgeous Mourning

Gorgeous Mourning

Alice Jones

Apogee Press
Berkeley · California
2004

Acknowledgments

For K.—I knew it was water I longed for.

Gratitude to Carol Snow for her stupendous expenditure of time and care. Thanks to Ed Smallfield and Alan Goldfarb for their comments on the manuscript. And thanks to the editors who published these poems or earlier versions of them.

Absomaly: Bode, Coo
The Colorado Review: Assent
Crab Orchard Review: Issue
Five Fingers Review: Auger, Conceal, Halt, Know, Open
Fourteen Hills: Reply, Ring
The Harvard Review: Log, Pass, View
Quarterly West: Hurry, Mourn
Slope: Concentrate, Escape, Forge, Gallop, Seize, Vacate
Upstairs at Duroc (Paris): Blend, Enter, Inquire, Lose
ZYZZYVA: Brandish, Journey, Leap, Sever

An excerpt from the manuscript won the 2001 Robert H. Winner Award from the Poetry Society of America.

Book design by Philip Krayna Design, Berkeley, California.
www.pkdesign.net

ISBN 0-9744687-1-1. Library of Congress Catalog Card Number 2003113639.

Published by Apogee Press, Post Office Box 8177, Berkeley CA, 94707-8177.
www.apogeepress.com

Table of Contents

Log

Afternoon of slumber, logging dreams on the mind's dusty screen. Where did it come from, that cartoon sleep of sawing timber? We lumber up from depths, wrestling with sunlight, uncrusting our eyes. An unrecognized timbre of voice loudly shouting something new, limber of tongue, loose of syllogism. Don't rest, write it down. We're up to no good, barking up the wrong tree. That story where Wynken, Blynken and Nod sail forth cloudy-headedly, navigating the sky in a wooden clog, star-lit. The recording angel's lost her book and deeply sleeps the day away in dreams of woods, those papery trees, everything rustling.

Enter

Spring is in full swing: the house is swarming with electricians. I've fallen in love with two lips. Not a peep from the past. Everything, now. Our new gate light; new doorbell sings— come in.

View

A day with no more purpose than any other, perched and looking, the curlew's call, a fever waning: what's in purview now? After ginger and curcuma, parched and reaching for anything to satisfy a thirst that's larger than this lake. What do you propose? After the cat-fight, fur flew around the yard for days until someone procured it to line a nest, only the best for her new eggs. The winning cat, now on curfew, bathes on her blue sill with a purr, viewing the courtyard, a few daffodils, also with no purpose, blooming.

Open

What we have in hand is a bunch of questions. Don't pander to common sense. We're beyond that, not that it's pandemonium we're after; it's just—be Pandora: open the box—there might be hell or the next pandemic, there might be a panda lazily chewing her bamboo, maybe Pindar penning odes (if they had pens then), or the grand panjandrum telling us what's what. Don't push the panic button, just look.

Whirl

After oral surgery, half-waking, woozy, what the room does
and refuses not to do. That bumper sticker, *visualize whirled
peas.* Children making themselves spun-drunk twirl until they
fall, lie laughing in the grass. You come in from the car
carrying your work things, set them down, remember what
you forgot, turn and go back out. Gyroscopes, tops. Dizzily,
she tried to quote the thing from Engels learned in her Marxist
youth about freedom being the appreciation of necessity, but
got it tangled up with the mother of invention. We never see
Jamie, home from college for the holidays, every time we turn
around she's gone snow-boarding or to breakfast at the Thai
Temple, for a run up in Tilden, to a party or another movie or
a friend's house for dinner. In the newspaper, a map of space
junk, all the dead satellites circling the globe, a thick belt. The
rabbit spins on his axis, Shiva-like, small fur god, before landing.
The smoothie, my blended raspberry and banana lunch, cold
in my stomach. Listening to the impeachment hearings, all
those cameras again. That waltz we never mastered.

Reply

Dear one, remember our moon-set walk across the trestle bridge, trees full of parasitic mistletoe? Are you still eating beef tendon and gristle soup with noodles? My unattended yard now blooms with purple thistles. They fired guided missiles from the mainland, pointed like flying fish, landing with a piscatory splash off-shore. Piss-poor shots, I'd say. The pistil is to stamen as mortar is to pestle, as heart is to well-aimed pistol, as I am to your epistle. Missing you, yours.

Bridle

During the rehearsal dinner the unreined ring-boy demonstrated a karate kick and his shoe flew, lodging in the atrium's huge chandelier. The grandfather of the bride seemed bewildered by his cummerbund and when he walked down the aisle, we saw he had cinched it too tightly. The grandmother looked askance at white for a second wedding. Seeing one guest without a tie, the father of the bride bristled, pulling his chin inward like an angry horse. When the music changed to the familiar march, knowing our cue, we all rose.

Gallop

Beset by the haves and have-nots, the shoeless burnt feet, rosy-lipped babies in back slings, the milk running over, a flat dog that someone not looking ran over, infants in shelters, infants without, the stories we were told, all their forest unfoldings, the ones we were not, held in a brown velvet bag tied with gold braid, dawn bats flying by at all angles, a pink sow, the bellowing calves and the calves' calves who will issue forth into plenitude and slaughter, all of us blissfully tail-swishing down the same chute.

Vacate

Please drop the topic of cancer. Travel becomes us. The globe's widened belly. Erogenous, earth's tropical zones, balmy wind after thunder storm, creaky roller coaster on drenched beach. One erroneous cell here or there, proteins slide along the double helix correcting lapses. Erasure. Coast line. The scooped-out abdomen. So many organs removable, the rich purples covered in pink silk. Slipshod. Waltzing barefoot. Let's take off. Where to?

Forge

Full of dreams and oranges, trying to forge a consciousness to meet the day, what were those converging images?—the Yangtze's Three Gorges before they were dammed; a matador gored by the triumphant bull, his livid face, the veins engorged; Curious George engaged in eating his own fleas; a host of angels pouring forth "Gloria in excelsis"; a furnace, its dipper full of molten glass poured, blown, cooled, so color and forms emerge. I forget what it all meant. Gorgeous morning.

Blind

The men would get up long before dawn to take my brother hunting, to sit in the dark, waiting. I'd wait for them to come home and gut their kill on the garage floor—duck, brown rabbits, bright-feathered pheasants, the hidden insides laid open to light. I needed to know something about death, how the feathers lie still, no breath, unseeing eyes. I didn't want to think how the buckshot we'd later taste got scattered through the tough meat. I didn't want to see blood. But I loved to look.

Seize

I'll tell you sometime when we're vis-à-vis about the ease of
memorizing dynasties, the pedigrees of poets, how Tang, the
apogee, floats into Sung; those liquid trees in scrolls, eerie in
the fog, or snow-covered bamboo teasing us with thoughts of
Spring; we're on our knees trying to take in time wider than
Lake Erie—you sneezed, we tried to squeeze it, don't believe
it, my freezing carp of the day.

Lose

The disappearance of plain song. A narrowing aperture. Always complaining, the plaintiff lost his suit. Just trying to sustain himself on grievance, left hungry. Plainly grieving for what you never had: naked rapture, nature's raptors. Time's plane taking off into our unclaimed future. Plaintively looking back at what we can't recapture.

Slip

Wanting lower down, she knelt before the vomiting made her faint. Enclosed, the blue rejection slip. How the tongue has a mind of its own: the psychic mechanism gets around itself so meaning has a sidekick. His grave face, the corners of the mouth pulling; he wanted to get himself caught shoplifting, that shame. His grandmother picked up every banana peel she found on the street. They had to park the boat somewhere. The day the elastic gave and my slip fell way down below the skirt, she was sure I was dying.

Journey

Drawn by incense and its ashes, crossing deserts, red ants, nomads in tents, to oases of wells, dates, ten cents a kilo, veiled cousins, sense and its discontents, camels in tens herded by incensed teenagers in jeans, the only trees for miles. I'm drawn by a scent, by sin, sensing the intense lure of the unseen: here's looking for you.

Mourn

Ordinary, because everyone is full of loss. Still not awake, coffee and morning bun. Sweet and sticky, the things that stay with you: the French horn you didn't learn to play, animals left alone too long, the daypack you never sent to Kashmir, a return call from the airport which would have been one more before he died. Lovelorn. Unformed, words for what's gone down the drain. I thought we would have years. At day's end, a shroud of damp gray air, mournful quail notes fading.

Hurry

A kiss flew by—whissh—like time. It is what it is: a fissure in
the present. Our tissues—skin, fascia, the trusses of bone,
issue us into risible nothing: there—the skeleton's forced grin
is new, we look possessed. Dissolution. A dancing Vishnu.
Gone—I'll miss you.

Brandish

My grandfather staked up dahlias along the neighbor's fence, his way of declaring war. She paraded her big turquoise necklace to every party. My mother said, "You start with a good rug, then build the room around it." After stopping in Egypt to ride camels around the pyramids with his mother, my other grandfather, the minister, traveled to China in 1903 and brought back a cloisonné vase which sits, dented, on my dresser. A smile, the exhibiting of teeth and of intent. At the end of her reading, she closed her book with a flourish that affected us like a musketeer's low bow, waving a feathered hat in one wide swoop. In order to make one's point, it isn't necessary to shoot, merely to display the gun.

Rifle

The thieves riffled through my top dresser drawer, spilling silk scarves on the floor. My great-grandmother's ruby, gone, and the stifling amethyst from my parents which arrived during our rift when I was living with riffraff in the woods. Aimed at another sort of life, I misfired. Who needs jewels? Still, rifled through with familial thoughts which backfire at inopportune moments—I'm ambushed. For years I'd gone around insisting I was robbed.

Jackknife

A question of opening and closing. I bend down to pick up the spoon still ringing on the tile floor. Springing up, lofting the pike into air, chest to thigh, wanting to go straight up but trying to miss the board coming down, to enter clean and vertical. Timing is everything. On Route 5, deep tule fog fooled everyone again. Thirty eight cars piled up behind a truck angled across the freeway. They know this happens and still they go, eyes open, speeding into it.

Wonder

I don't have a clue. I thought I knew more than that. Think it over, chew morsels slowly. Maybe something will unfold like those embryos, slowly morphing into form that can breathe. Or a slew of tumor cells piling up and going on beyond the edges, unruly. The mind, off on a gallop, now stops by the pool to graze, chew its cud, to admire round-eyed, the wide ether blue. Happy fool.

Inquire

Keeping current, Kirin, C-span, to see what's occurring today in the seesawing currency markets. We incur rent. See? It's up again. The catacombs are full and we can't see a cure for occupying space. Curious, the curriculum of progress. The obsolete curricle, gone; two horses left over, currycombed and put to field. Currants, seedless, how do they do it? Electricity, explain it to me. Did it ever occur to you? Questioning, we're pulled under by currents of a cursive sea.

Reveal

Open the door in the tree, step into some unapparent side of
the self—the moon gone under, reflected back onto your
earthly eyes—look, the beyond—the Tao moves the other way,
neolithic jade—material moonlight and semen, silk, plateau
to the Yellow River and the sea, flood plain, if you choose to
go, be happy for a place without ground where the sound of
alarm won't reach you. Early morning of veined granite
crevices. Afternoon's rock-baked lizards run back to the center
of earth and hide in their molten places where no eye will
intrude. Evening—the unseen vibrating in circles waited all
those hours to emerge; imagine—your feet without earth,
where every tunnel in is naked flight.

Plumb

With aplomb, that's how he handles things—there's a dash to him, with sleeves and no side glances, cool as a plum in the refrigerator, not closed up, open and quick, he ascertains depths. The cat, plump yet springy as a lamb, sniffs at the applesauce, ambles away. Unflappable dancers stretching lean limbs in front of the mirror, from perpendicular to low *port de bras*, take pleasure in their limber reach. At Home Depot, an abundance of shoppers, appliances, piled up lumber, plumb lines and drain parts, she drops her hanging geranium in its planter to applause, and with equanimity she bows. The old yard abounded with plum trees, in June fruit dropping like small leaden bombs from full limbs, and the yard would become crumbly toast under an ample layer of plum jam. Then bumblebees.

Believe

I don't. Thunderheads and forgetfulness. That's what we're full of today. Electricity wandering around. No Thor of the clouds breathing down on us. No Osiris or Zeus. No transmigration of anything but molecules. Organic compounds unglued and looking for home. I found you. Statistically, it was against the odds, my odd one. Do we need a larger shape to nestle into? O thou my comfort for thousands of days, on earth and not beyond. I think it's like that. Bound by the edges of one life. What time weaves into us and us into. Should we call that knot the mystical rose of being? Let's not call it anything at all.

Recognize

Science is the scion of seeing. Darwin worked it out: the sequence of lumpy turtles, blue-footed boobies, bumpy iguanas in the Galapagos, a zion of creatures who unbecame. They were sighted from The Beagle with a sigh, hence our map of species, divided by the scimitar of time, each one a sequin in the eye of what we know.

Stray

Unless I splash, no one notices how I eat until, at a restaurant, the crumb sweeper comes around and spends all his time in front of me. The black cat never came back. At Thai dinner, squid salad too hot, flushed, sweating, you wipe your scalp with a cloth napkin and all your hair stands up on end. She wanted me to join the Junior League as she did, but I had my eye on a communist splinter group.

Stuff

Go dive into the box of chocolates. Pick open a little divot in the carapace, find the coconut in order to avoid it. (That nugatory map inside the lid never helps.) What is nougat anyway? The search was for caramels, nuggets of gold snuggled into the crenelated wrapping papers. Remember Lucy's assembly line, how it accelerates until each box nudges the next and there's no way to nestle each confection into its brown crinoline? She's helpless in the struggle to keep up, cramming candy inside her apron, her cheeks: a race with time that's always lost.

Climb

Inclement weather again, let's stay inside and lament the loss of sunshine. Maybe shade is more merciful, no blinds on the clerestory windows. Is that what your uncle meant? We should find a clematis, send it to spiral up the trellis, to clench tiny footholds upwards out of the cement terrace and bloom there in its element. Columbine combining with shasta daisies by the stairs where you fell, poor cleaved ankle, meatless, not much to splint it. Climbing: everyone wants up. Was that the Incas' intent, building Machu Picchu so high to speak the language of the sun? Have I mentioned the reach of the hummingbird's tongue, slick filament? My climate of confusion? This climacteric isn't sensible, have clemency.

Sever

She only wanted leg and not the chicken thigh so tried politely to disarticulate them with her fork. Each time I really understood, she screamed at me—"Back off!" Wanting them not to seed the whole yard, picking dandelions before they bloom. She was there to cut the cord of the baby she was adopting. The rabbit sliced through the refrigerator cord with just one bite. Students interviewed the muscular young man who had just had his cancerous arm removed; the tricky part, he said, was learning how to walk, because it threw his balance off. "Time's up."

Fascinate

It's not the taste of mouse the cat loves, but the way the mouse moves.

Circle

Spanning the cracks with pitons and ropes, still climbing into ourselves across gullies and streams, the past, happy lawns full of swans and flamingoes, tarred piers out on pylons. A fish caught with no bait, a yank snags him. In nylons or clogs and tortoise shell hair clip, I land in your sphere where pi longs for its circle: the snake bites its tail, a grin on the python displaying his scales.

Ring

Listen mister, no more hysteria—just kiss her. Not speaking
has its history, smoldering like old bugs, e. coli, listeria. Build
your nest here, not the Waldorf Astoria. Mysterious and twiny
as hair, wisteria dangles from the trellis. Leafless. We thought
the twisted form was killed by frost, but now two furry buds,
small balled fists, turn misty blue, unfold. Some bells on the
mute jester's hat.

Halt

Surprised, rounding the corner, to see a peacock running down The Alameda, tail furled, arresting traffic with his presence. Some forms of matter never enter other phases naturally, stay gas or liquid unless you cool them down approaching absolute zero, which you never get to. Lying on our new deck, looking up at stars, I thought your breathing stopped. One drop of olive oil hanging, held there, on the bowl's glass lip. Wondering what it meant—the lame, the halt, the blind...

Disintegrate

Compose yourself. With the mind in compartments? Or with everything loose, on the hoof. Comportment they used to call it, a girl's good behavior. No time off. When is a mind complete? What about a mind ajar, incapable of communication, maybe aphasic, maybe vegetative, awake but responding to none of the world's come-ons, thought without a compass? The commodious regions of nonsense, have we gone there? The night we first saw the comet, we walked out the red door and found the clearly visible thumbprint smudged in the northwest. Feeling the cat's kittens inside her belly, first a lumpiness, then discrete shapes, heads and small parts become palpable. People would comply with the request to bring their discarded Christmas trees to the high school for a bonfire, combustion so intense the still-draped tinsel would melt, embers smoldered for days before the heap became completely ash. We emptied the compost from its bin, it still holds a shape, to our surprise, the cube of stuff sprouting a layer of green grassy hair. Comb out your rapunzel plait across the calico pillow. She sallies forth, decamps with the knowledge of decomposition folded in her back pocket, as we all do. Tell me confidentially—are we calm? Are we completely at sea?

Flout

Those crows. Not wearing a tie to his niece-in-law's black tie ceremony. At the Berkeley High graduation one boy flung open his red gown to show he was wearing nothing underneath and a girl in a tube-top began to jump up and down until her breasts bounced free: our graduate's great-aunt said in too-loud Cantonese, "Those are very bad children." He learned how to fail even the simplest exam, "Really," he said, "it's an art." During our silence, a motorcycle revs up outside then tears off. Nude at the wrong beach.

Emanate

That sort of espionage you conduct, looking for radiances on behalf of... How to unlock the little door? Did you put the car keys in the bell jar? Might as well throw them down the sink, artesian well. That's not Cartesian logic, but it's a swell idea. Let's put them on a barge, float them off across the Carquinez Straits. What was it Aquinas said? Never an equation, you merely describe the current equilibrium. When you get it almost right, that feeling of elation.

Blend

I like those cappuccino drinks whirled up with ice. Out on the sidewalk at Royal Coffee, we sat at a green metal table watching coffee drinkers mingle with homeless. The man in black who wears a turban, one long earring, and carries all he owns in an overflowing pack, has a bench to himself because he stares. The man all in red has the driveway to himself because he says "motherfucker" and pokes the air with long arms. Later at home, our sometimes-family sleeps inside stucco, I'm not used to hearing the toilet down the hall flush at 3 a. m.—our water flows out to the bay to mix with everyone's.

Impel

Nearly intimidated by his intimation (just a whiff, really) of enormous knowledge, we're left meditating on the imminent arrival of our comeuppance. Such imbroglios should be immaterial to our pride. You might think that our certainty of operating at an intermediate level would immediately terminate all fears of immense ignorance, however our concern is not mitigated in the least. Perhaps our timidity is augmented by his inimical demeanor or his inimitable sneer, and so we decide that his presence is an immiscible element in our sphere. And rather than imitating the impotent tortoise, we find ourselves imagining an impetuous emigration.

Flit

Afternoon's short reach, we never arrived but oh, we traveled. Titillated? I've told you all this before, a memory on the tip of the tongue. Wisps of fog coming in over the hazy headlands, the inland heat fritters them away. A precipitate of what? Your slow wave sleep unravels itself, conscious again of what's left of daylight. Sorry old thing in your skin bag. They tell me I fibrillate. Another tribulation. The search for unnamed fritillaries is never over.

Bolt

A businessman man got on BART at 19th, sat next to me and finished eating his burger by 12th Street. For earthquakes, they anchored into our foundation then ran steel cables up two floors. Over and over I urged my parents, and finally they agreed to send me to boarding school for 11th grade. Lightning struck, cracked, and the aluminum dog dish at my feet flipped and flew across the driveway. A paisley challis laid out across the table; which way to lay out the pattern? Hesitating not long enough before making the first cut.

Glean

Who said bright wires humming? The nerves are dumb worms, flat, silky in tensile sheathes. Packed into bone tunnels, bundled, a harvest unreaped, we gather together, take it all in. And yes, there's the eye: nervous layers, photochemicals, an invisible nacre glows in the dark, pearly dish full of vitreous humor. Who's laughing? I see you like this: radar to neural network to memory and what I expect. It's kind of hard to get you with this meshwork blinding us, binding us, oh well, we do what we can.

Coo

Your face in firelight, indigo on one side, glutinous yellow on
the other. You must be the moon. Our dark sides adhere, skin
to skin, new music, Brazilian and zoo-dark, embers' spooky
light lapping your legs, the ceiling, your no-belly. Dinner of
couscous, now the true you. The fountain murmurs, a few
splays of bamboo, Chusquea coronalis, remind us of tropics,
moist circles, what the lips do, gluing.

Issue

Going forth towards the far shore, beyond everything namable, to a place where we were never children, no father to mark his thumbprint onto our foreheads, no identical shape of small toe to claim us as his, maybe creatures instead with brown fur, the right thing to keep warm when you're out on a limb, where we like to pretend we seldom are though it's actually our everyday address, farm of the unseen, we're fathering shoots out of furrows of time rumpled and collapsing in earthy crumbs: that's how we're grounded.

Bristle

In the car, she reached over to stroke his thigh, he pulled
away. The radio was saying "Skirmishes broke out along the
border" and he wanted to argue causes, economy or culture.
She thought of the Dalai Lama's one naked shoulder, a life of
feeling the wind in an armpit, exile.

Swallow

Eons. The hummingbird dipped, entered the flower's bell, hung there. The lines across her face intersect, fine mesh consuming the belle she was. On the clover field where we grew up, a multiplex. Storm coming, the first dark edge of shadow engulfs us. Tu Fu in "Dreaming Li Po": "After you die, I swallow your voice." The mecurial pool, welcoming.

Heat

Slow your tempo, take my temperature. Fevered, we and the big flowering cactuses are temporarily roasting in the Big Sur hills. The bizarreness of those temporal lobe seizures which follow no template. A rare bellowing temper has tempered us like steel. Am I the temptress in the teapot? You intemperate man, so responsive, love noises. Afterwards, sitting hand to temple looking out at the temporal flux of water. Hiking up from Bon Tempe Lake, is Mt. Tam really supposed to look like a sleeping woman?

Confiscate

The teacher said don't play with clay and took it away. She made us write a hundred times, or was it a thousand, "I will not play with clay in Symphony." Even if my ears were occupied, I had nothing to do with my hands. I liked the way you could press the clay down on a Sunday comic strip, then peel it back, bring away an impression of Dagwood stealing a nap. My fingers seemed to have ideas of their own about form, not forcing it out of the stuff so much as calling it forth. Older, I thought of becoming a sculptor and was encouraged. But something in me said no.

Improve

I won't make muffins on the trail, although it would be easy, equipped with Bisquick. He'd better quit it, whistling like that. I'm tired of the ubiquitous mosquitoes biting in our tent, although they like him better. He says just swat them. What about karma? Then we'll come back for more, he says, better and better, that's how this life is getting.

Scale

The floorboards are curling, so scaly in the morning, one eye that falls open in sleep, dry dreams, the vast rippled desert encroaching, oases sanded under, longing growing deep like the rooted palms, fronded, subsisting. Bedouins sweeping the drifting sand out their doors ululate, high pitch, seeing their homes will soon be consumed. Dreams of a never-seen ocean, frothy, whirling winds, birds ascend in their gyre, a dream spun of thin thread, whole cloth, where does it come from, knowing what a desert of water would look like, landlocked, improbable sea.

Sink

Your stomach falls as the rapid transit zooms downhill going under the bay for seven minutes and you race along thinking how many feet of rock and mud and bay lie over your head, the weight of water there, unseen. The pot hole swallowed two lanes of traffic. We'd throw bottle caps into the deep end and they'd flutter as they descended. Oblivious to time, we dove to retrieve them over and over, until the sun would get low and our mother would call us home to dinner, then she'd stand there with the dishes she'd wash and wash.

Expunge

Never having suckled a child, she thought breasts were a waste of time to begin with. After the mastectomy, she refused to remember what his love letters said, or where they were hidden. Her chest prepped for radiation, she wondered what to do about those purple-red marks at the pool. Tamoxafen to block her estrogen, gesso to paint over her old canvases.

Dread

That constant feeling of peril in the mountains—avalanche.
Let's go anyway, pack a lunch and sit side by side on a fallen
stump. I have a hunch you'll like this spinach sandwich. At
home we paved over the nasturtiums, we gave a brunch and
put the flowers in fruit salad. The cat lunged—a finch in her
clenched jaw. Offer the branch of peace. No one's biting. We
imagine earthquakes, typhoons, lava launching us out the
door—fast. You crave a ranch where no intruder will bother
us, no news of calamity, however, the crunched sprig of danger
always parslies the morning.

Concentrate

How they get orange juice inside the can. The cat curls in the corner, her ears twitch following something we can't see. Purple darkness gathers on the eastern hills, grows denser, seems to pull in more of itself magnetically. The recipe said reduce the wine sauce by half. We saw the owl high up in a cedar, watching. Words going somewhere new, someplace I don't know how to follow, trying to find the limb from which to branch. Jessie doing logarithms, what her forehead does, rehearsing lines it won't wear for forty years.

Attend

Outdoors, our first frost in nine years was crystallizing; the tender of plants, pre-occupied, knew as we spoke that the schizostylus sagged, the zalusianskya drooped, the protea set down its arms. Each rare species, the tendrils would be brown by morning, all those colors sent from the hot continent, some grown from seed, seen through infancy into full bloom. Maybe he was figuring what could be sprayed into ice, saved by glaze. Tightening a tendon in his jaw he'd said, "It's a risk, it happens." Held captive by our talk, he was elsewhere, each tall spike, each bulb, the tender splays of orange and yellow, dying now behind his eyes.

Choose

Granted three wishes, precious few, what will you ask for?
World peace or at least non-aggression, good posture,
dancing dervishes, hot knishes? Never mind, be judicious,
close the refrigerator door on those delicious leftovers, two-
dish-catfish, a mish-mash in Tupperware, go do dishes, you
can't grieve for everything, choose your own misses and
losses; the pink sponge, a few swishes will please you: clean
counter tiles, polished glasses and brass figures, new Ganeshas,
blue Krishna, dancing Siva, pernicious Kali, we don't need the
gods' permission, and so to bed.

Mooch

She invented a definition form, with leaps; I leapt and ended up with verbs. I used to meet with a teenager who after a couple of months got a haircut that matched mine. My stepfather had an airedale named Lulu, greedy pooch, who would sneak up behind me at breakfast, lunge and steal my toast. My psychotic uncle used to lean over, much too close, and say, "Give us a smooch."

Augur

A knotty question. We ought to trace an answer. You know tea and its leaves. I want ground coffee, not tea. Naughty boy, gnawing the teething ring, clear through. It's coming: the year ought-ought. Increasing awe. Now tease me again.

Organize

Conquistadors of imagination, let's pin it down, make a system,
cross-reference. In unison. We never flew the Concorde to Paris
and now it's grounded. Bring the camcorder to the Grand
Concourse. Trace all those particular dreads, the screech of the
subway, peach brick parapets, the water bottle that empties
itself, the floating face on the wall, ghostly and misshapen.
Remember *Amarcord?* Was that the one with breasts?
Ventricular peppers, a pint of memory, a dash of curry,
remove and seed the core, serve warm. Oops, the sudden
floor. A klutz of course. Chaotic. Another slip, proof of your
failure to arrange, sweep out the corners. Curious mind.
Order—even this can be conquered.

Elide

Pink field of skin, Elysian, the baby's bottom, ripe apricots, faint fur. Leave off the diaper. Elision. The tongue's slip, writing its own mind, collision of intent with the unmeant. The Asian dermatologist removes a lesion. A few snips, ellipsis, a few sutures. Dysplasia begins at home, then it wanders, elusive cells. Your old dinghy, curled scales of beige paint, swings alee. Shun the high tides, the wild eddies, tack back into the shallow cove where eluvial shore eclipses peach sunset, that glow.

Conceal

Not writing. A dress without a belt. The locked drawer. Henna. Passing. The bedroom door. "There is no gold buried here." Hiding a bottle in the bottom of a trash bag. Landmines. The closet. The stash. Veil. Turtle shell, black tights, witness relocation, the Klan's hood, the baited hook, masquerade. I didn't want you to know. Allure: come find me.

Croon

for D

Florida palm trees with their unbreakable offspring, humid afternoon thunder, plethora of water and wishing she would wash us in it, over and over. She bathed our feet in turpentine when the blue men-of-war stung their nettled stings. Crib-bound, wanting, you have to imagine, invent a voice to answer, that shallow murmur of reply to every question—mm-hmm. They dropped us off at the orphanage when they went out. She told us this didn't mean anything. Acres of cribs. Head to toe, my brother and I shared. I'd hum us to sleep. He'd later say, "Your humming drove me nuts."

Recede

A rumbling bee on the cucumber, finding a clumsy foothold. A world set on wheels. Collapsed blossom, blood-caked, a fluid brine, slick once, its freshness gone into something other, fumbling down the hallways of long mirrors, the vale of tears, a mouse swimming, its feet go so fast, the little door. Eat me. An encounter with scent, with slippage, lost under the umbrella shade of datura, bats' wings folded, faint orange, an elusive whiff of umber nightmare. The little ova wash in and out, tide pools, anemones and their tubular fingers whishing around, all corners touched. We have salt here, bake it out on the drying rocks, time forms crystals on the boulders, we're eroding anyway, penumbra cast on summer afternoon, dumb shade and shades of meaning, fleeting, one touch, a buzz.

Twist

You asked me about looking at things askew, the view set on edge: a screw turns and nothing's quite the same. Usually we take the horizon as cue, what's up or down, the eye and brain talk to each other as quickly as anything, as quietly, as curious as necessary about a slew of things. We talked over a few eggs you scrambled in the crepe pan with chives. What else is new? Wondered if we could really fly to London, pictured Heathrow, the Tate, Big Ben, us, Kew Gardens, all these places you'd told me about when I didn't ask you. Your crooked smile saying, "Nice ass, cutie."

Plunge

Heavy lidded. Thoughts flit at the periphery of attention. A coast with hurried birds. One pulse, the base line, clitoral undercurrent. He told me the literal translation of his name—abundant benevolent rain. Spring rain. Cloud-lit. I knew it was water I longed for. And swimming, a preparation for this—the long littoral onset of immersion.

Pass

In the Punjab, no more tigers. What does the putamen do?
Or what is its repute? We hide the pudendum because of shame.
Reciting chapters from The Upanishads, standing upright on
the table, many writers were raised this way, a Pyrrhic victory
over silence, or do I mean a Punic war? Outside, the piñon
stands there with its nuts and needles. Many writers passed
away this way, prickly and fruitful, falling down when
their balance left them, lying floor-bound gazing upward,
talking on.

Leap

How we're always lunging, trying to catch up with real time. They've added leap years and now, leap seconds. Are we here yet? I love lapping people at the pool, it makes me feel so strong, their time, lost in my wake. It's almost tomorrow here. Can you catch up with the lip of it arcing through space? Leonid meteor shower, flung orbits, those swallowing collapsed places of dense matter, are we clean yet? Are we inside? Auspicious—to see a bat the dawn of our wedding day, because its name is a homophone for good fortune. And you, curled up beside me in your own time, dreaming of another continent in another language where each tone has meaning, a thought springs from you to me. Wait, I'll translate.

Escape

Be bold—roll down your sleeves, leave the trenches, be off to mountains where the leaves are goldening and it's cold at night, the one bright planet singing, "Don't grow old again, come breathe."

Bode

The Bardo, we're all in between. Live today... then up in smoke, someone's always drinking ashes. He read about Tibetan air burial, it takes a specialist to smash the bones so vultures eat even the marrow and the body's down to nothing in not much time. Who's waiting to be reborn? Thin border between this and that, the bordello of the world we were drawn into, willingly, but later, getting bored with excitements, bedded down in probabilities, even Manhattan ceases to amaze, it's just so much friction and decibels, a cold wind, hairy shrubs, chic northern wolfhounds, beet soup, every phone is portable as if they wanted to be reachable inside their caskets after the beep, where even the street bards and vindaloo won't wake them.

Fade

Mostly Mozart again in the *beaux-arts* symphony building, we
walk past homeless sleeping in folded cardboard cartons like
ancient boat parts, past old farts in baseball caps playing chess
at concrete tables in the windy park, on our way to taking in
the sung math, the bowed parts, now sun low, last light, our
dust falling, rising, one glimpse of multitude, invisible bosons,
almost lost, the motes' fine art.

Assent

The nude ascends to her lair, the nightgown hung on its cruel hook. On the stairs, uncle's photograph of Chinese children from behind going up steep stone steps, one with no shoes. Where to? No destination indicated in the dream of rising elevators, pitons, gliders, high-tech balloons. In the morning, new. Descending the oak stairs, past the gilded buddha, the wicker chair. Noon inclines into afternoon, lunch, the avenue widens, raspberry smoothie oozes into the noisy belly. Attention restored: yes—we say to all this—we're listening.

Home

That night we parked beside the bay, the landfill park by Golden Gate Fields after the races had ended, listening to Johnny Hartman in the dashboard's amber glow, and out of nowhere, interrupting, something by the window. Gone. Another. More. One by one the geese—out of darkness, so fast, as if falling down to skim the black water—going North. We could hear their wings before we saw them, whuph-whuph, so close they almost hit us, hurtling home.

PHOTO: Yoo-Chong Wong

ALICE JONES's books include *The Knot* which won the Beatrice Hawley Award in 1992 and *Isthmus* which won the Jane Kenyon Chapbook Award, both from Alice James Books. *Anatomy* was published by Bullnettle Press. *Extreme Directions (The fifty four moves of Tai Chi Sword)* was published by Omnidawn Press. She has been awarded fellowships by the Bread Loaf Writers Conference and the National Endowment for the Arts. Her poems have appeared in *Ploughshares, Denver Quarterly, Volt, Chelsea,* and *Best American Poetry of 1994.*